Time to Celebrate!

LET'S GO TO THE FAIR!

By Benjamin Proudfit

Please visit our website, www.garethstevens.com. For a free color catalog of all our high-quality books, call toll free 1-800-542-2595 or fax 1-877-542-2596.

Library of Congress Cataloging-in-Publication Data

Names: Proudfit, Benjamin, author.
Title: Let's go to the fair! / Benjamin Proudfit.
Description: New York : Gareth Stevens Publishing, 2020. | Series: Time to celebrate! | Includes index.
Identifiers: LCCN 2018044075| ISBN 9781538239025 (pbk.) | ISBN 9781538239049 (library bound) | ISBN 9781538239032 (6 pack)
Subjects: LCSH: Fairs–Juvenile literature.
Classification: LCC GT4580 .P76 2020 | DDC 394.26–dc23
LC record available at https://lccn.loc.gov/2018044075

First Edition

Published in 2020 by
Gareth Stevens Publishing
111 East 14th Street, Suite 349
New York, NY 10003

Editor: Kristen Nelson
Designer: Katelyn E. Reynolds

Photo credits: Cover, p. 1 Erik Isakson/Blend Images/Getty Images; p. 5 Monkey Business Images/Shutterstock.com; pp. 7, 24 (ribbon) acceptphoto/Shutterstock.com; p. 9 LightField Studios/Shutterstock.com; p. 11 ymgerman/Shutterstock.com; p. 13 Itsanan/Shutterstock.com; p. 15 ZikG/Shutterstock.com; pp. 17, 24 (pie) © iStockphoto.com/DNY59; p. 19 waldru/Shutterstock.com; p. 21 Andriy Solovyov/Shutterstock.com; p. 23 Iryna Liveoak/Shutterstock.com.

Printed in the United States of America

CPSIA compliance information: Batch #CS19GS: For further information contact Gareth Stevens, New York, New York at 1-800-542-2595.

Contents

It is time for the fair!
My family goes
every year.

Uncle Joe brings cows
to the fair.
They win ribbons!

There are other
animals, too.
Violet likes
the horses best.

Look at all the rides!
Kris goes on
the big slide.

1 2 3 4 5 6 7
1 3 4 5 6
NYC

Jack likes
the games best.

I win a prize!

There is a pie contest.
The blueberry pie wins!

1st

We see a band play
at night.

They play outside!

It is always fun
at the fair!
What will you do there?

STATE FAIR

Words to Know

pie

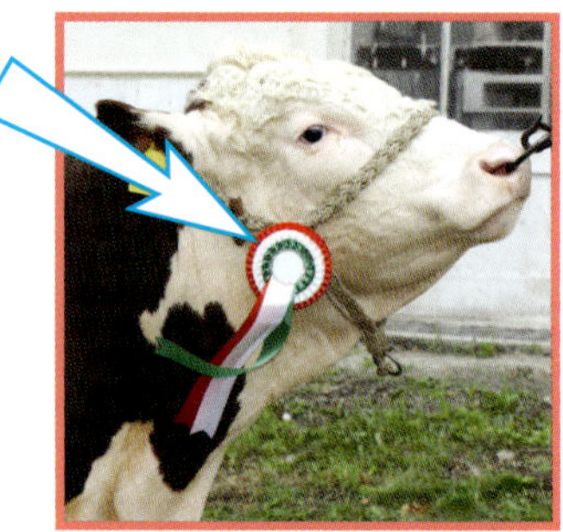

ribbon

Index